NIGHT SHIFT

DEBI GLIORI

RAZORBILL®

An Imprint of Penguin Random House LLC
Penguin.com

RAZORBILL & colophon is a registered trademark of Penguin Random House LLC.

First published in Great Britain by Hot Key Books, 2017
First published in the United States of America by Razorbill, an imprint of Penguin Random House LLC, 2017

ISBN 9780451481733

Printed in China

1 3 5 7 9 10 8 6 4 2

NIGHT SHIFT

DEBI GLIORI

I don’t know when it began.
Perhaps it drifted in at night like fog.

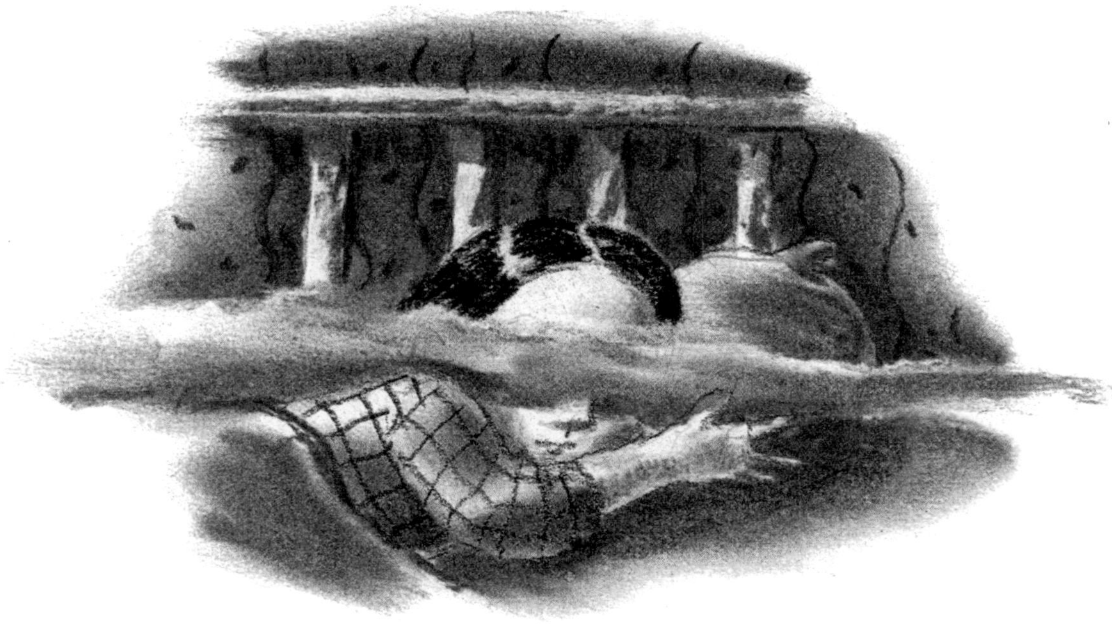

I felt tired.
All day long.

The fog rolled in every night,

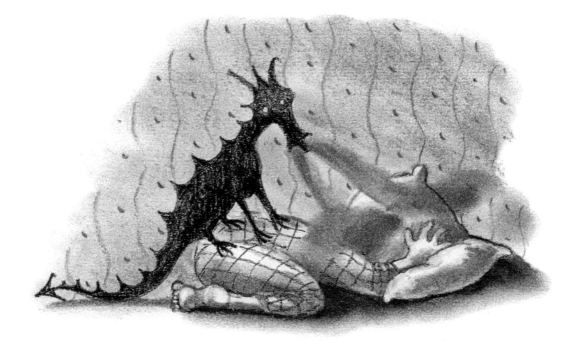

and during
the day too.

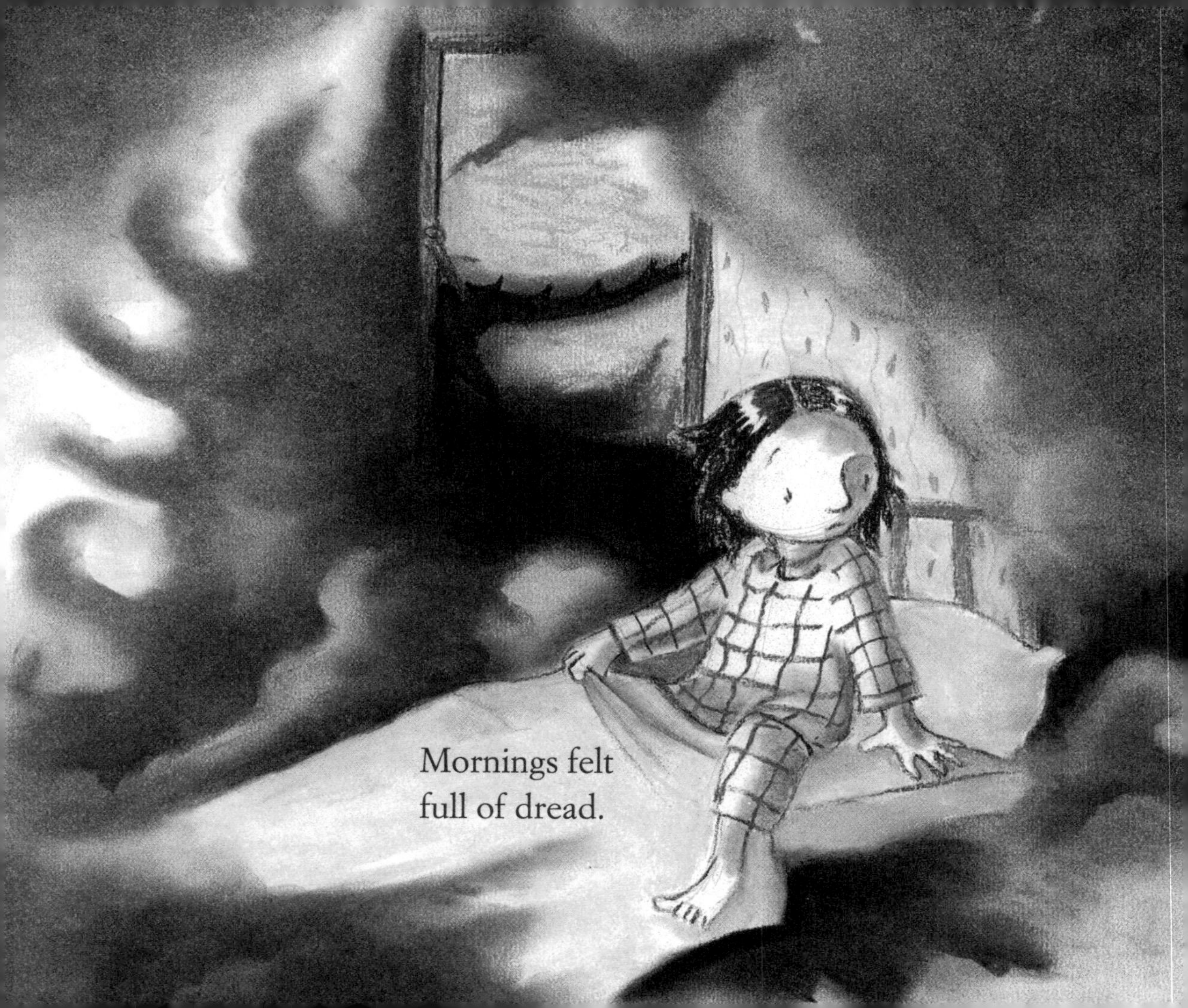
Mornings felt
full of dread.

Heart
hammering,
stomach
churning,

I felt
hollowed
out.

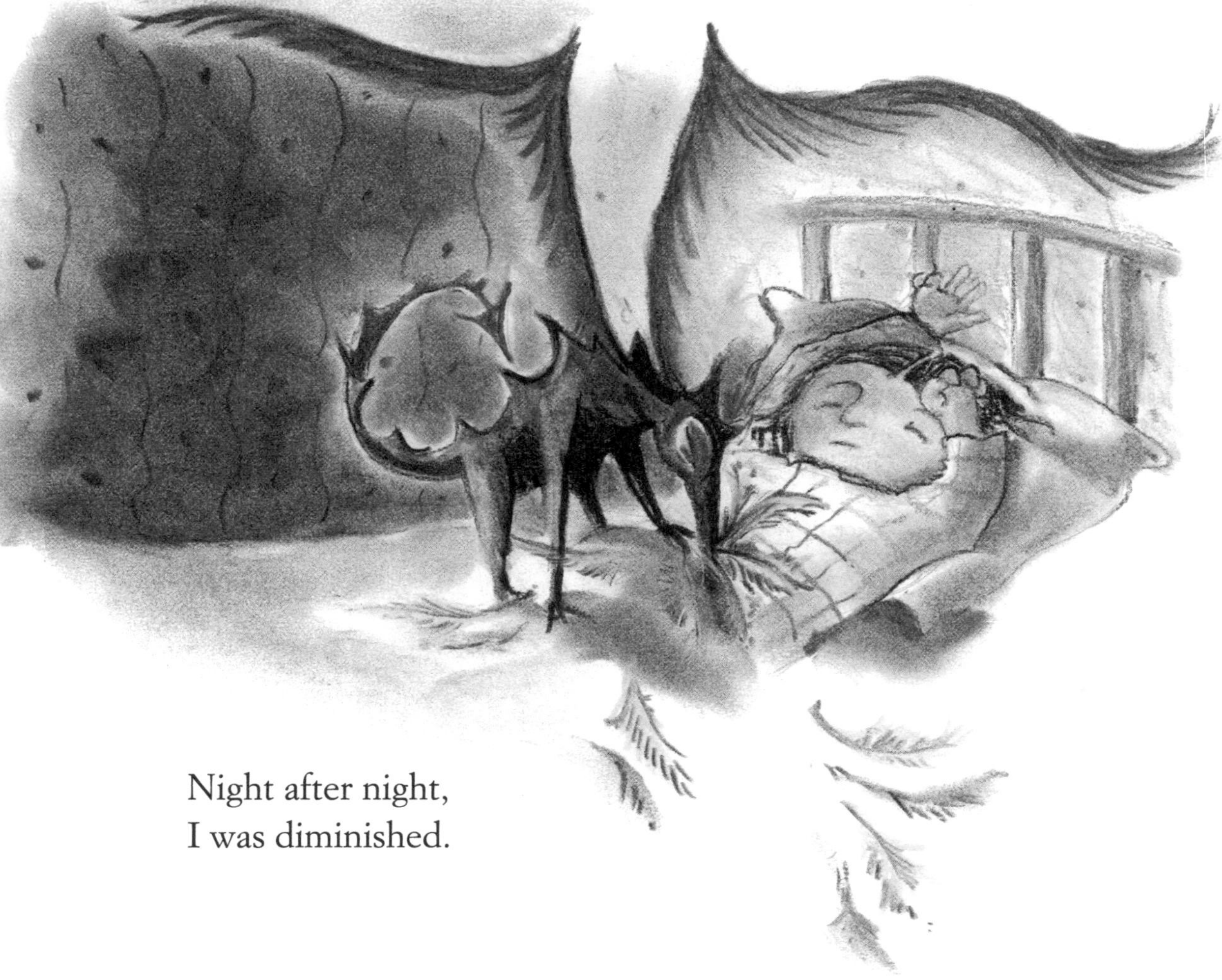

Night after night,
I was diminished.

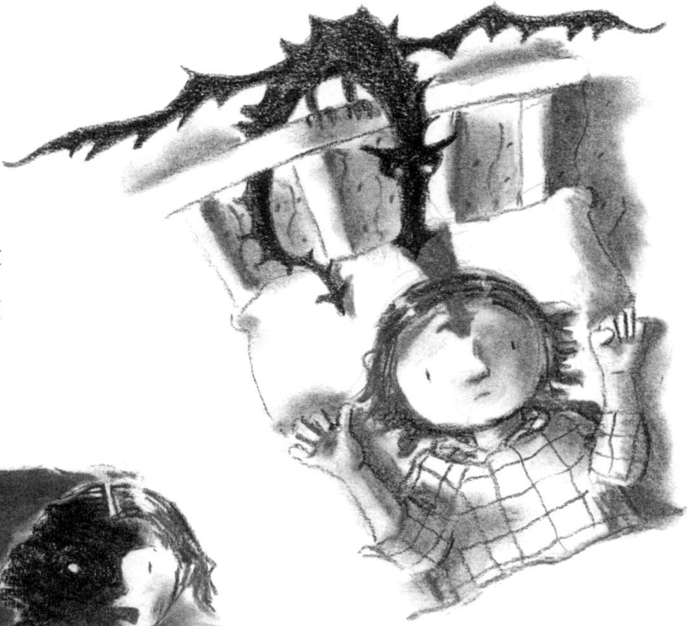

I awoke every night
afraid of something
I couldn't see.

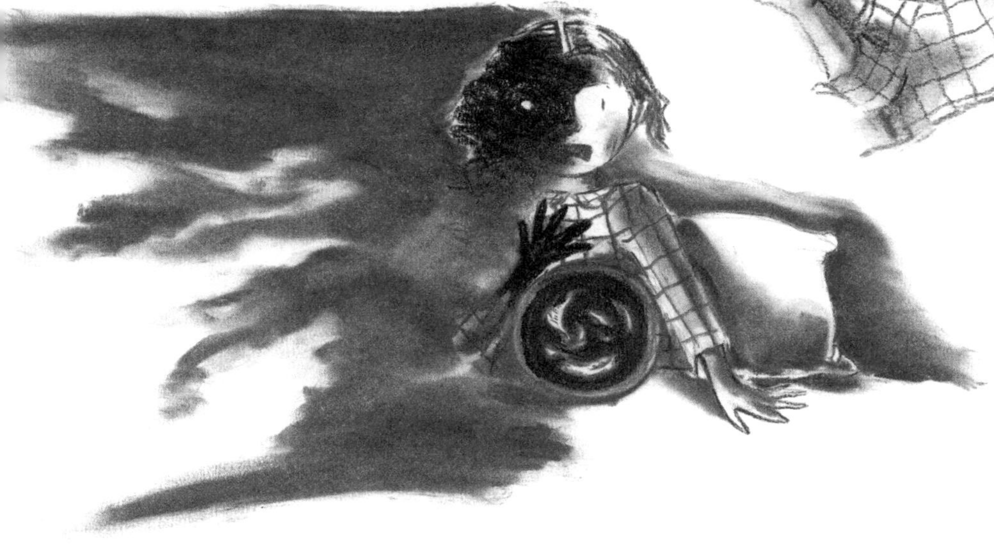

And one night
I didn't know
who I was any more.
I got up, looked in
the mirror, and saw
that I was ill.

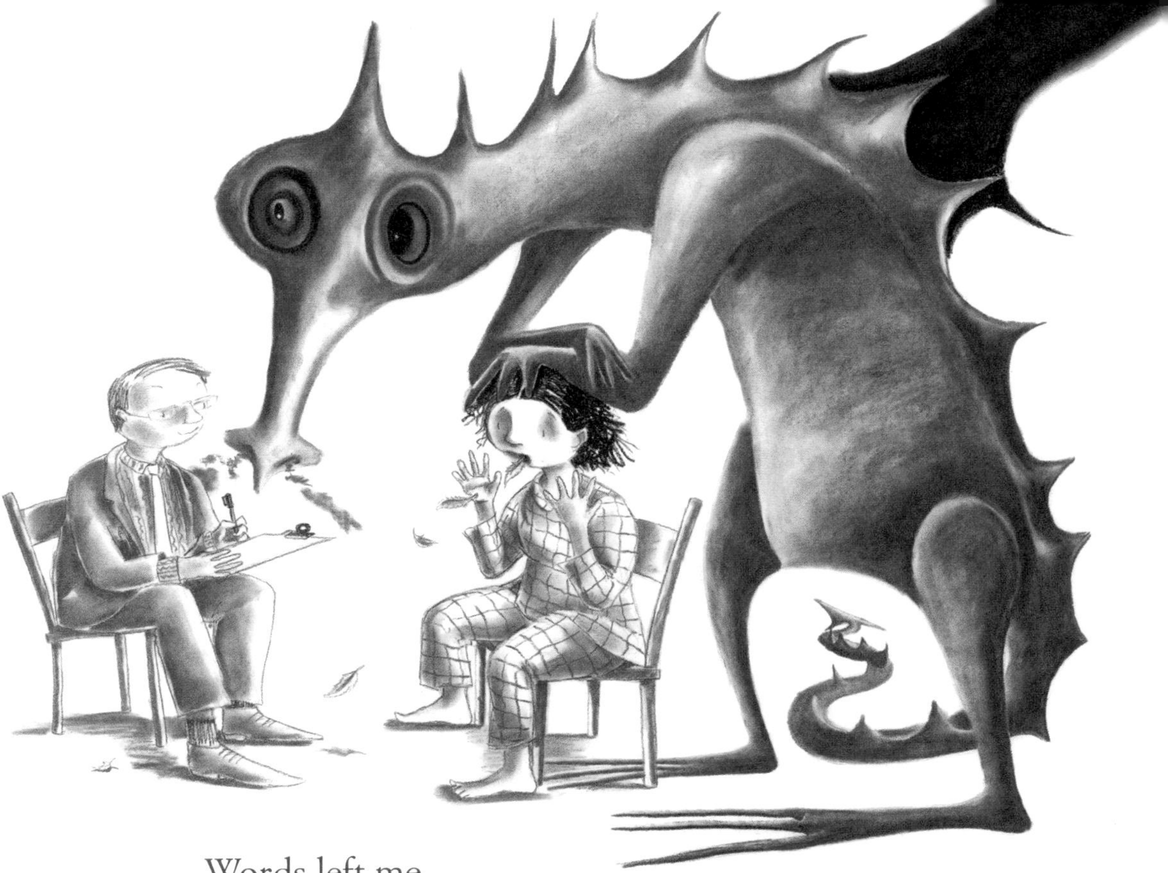

Words left me.
There was no language for this feeling.

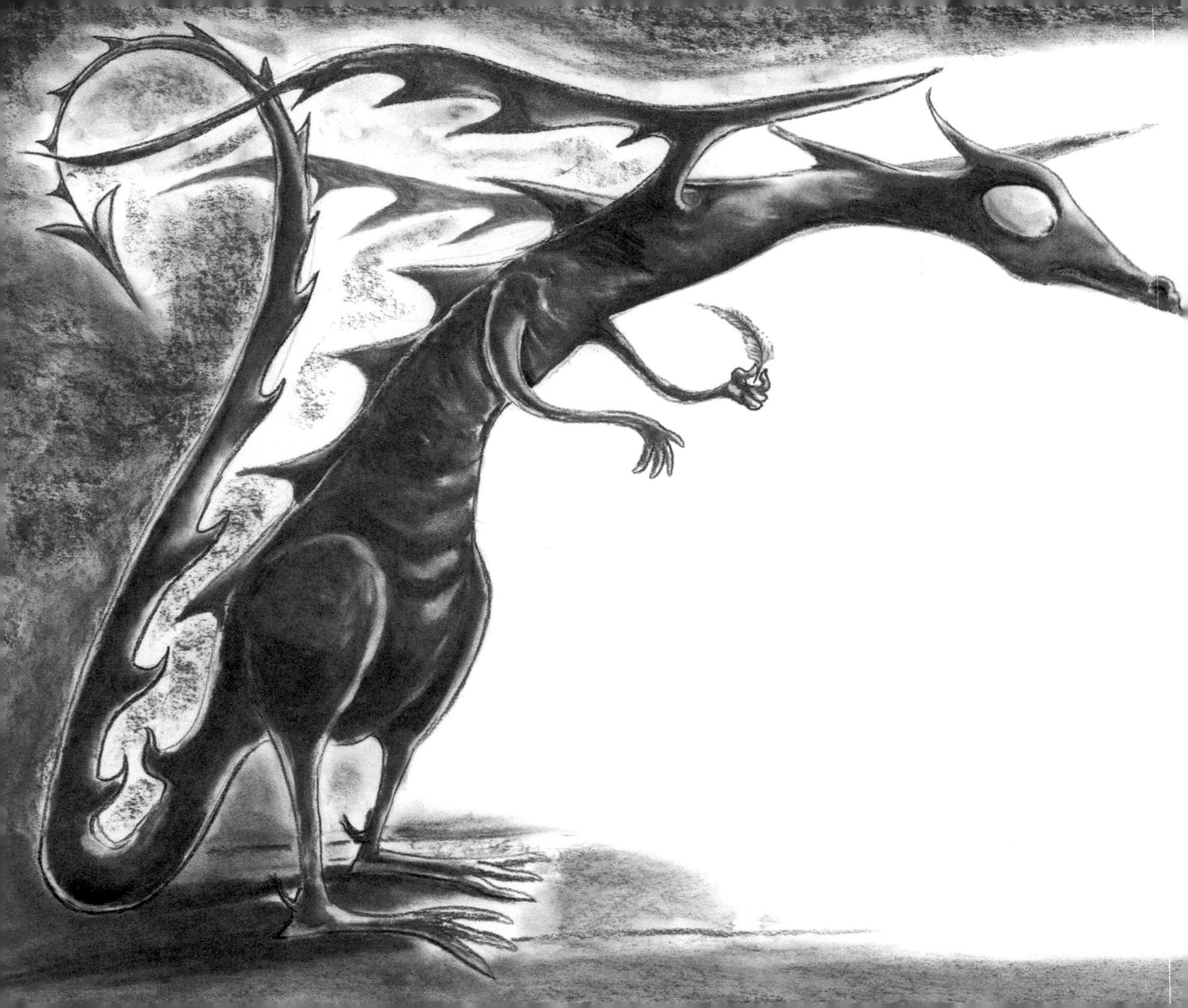

Lacking words, I tried to
draw a map to help me find
something I couldn't name.

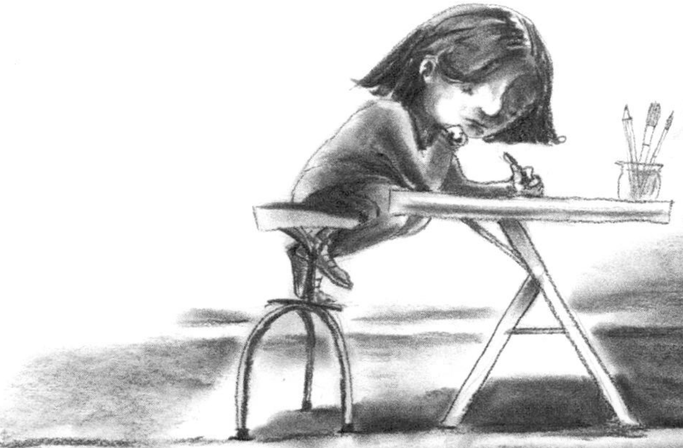

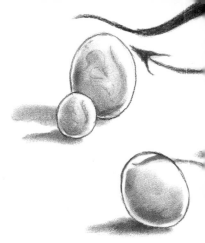

But I had lost my compass and without it any map was pointless.

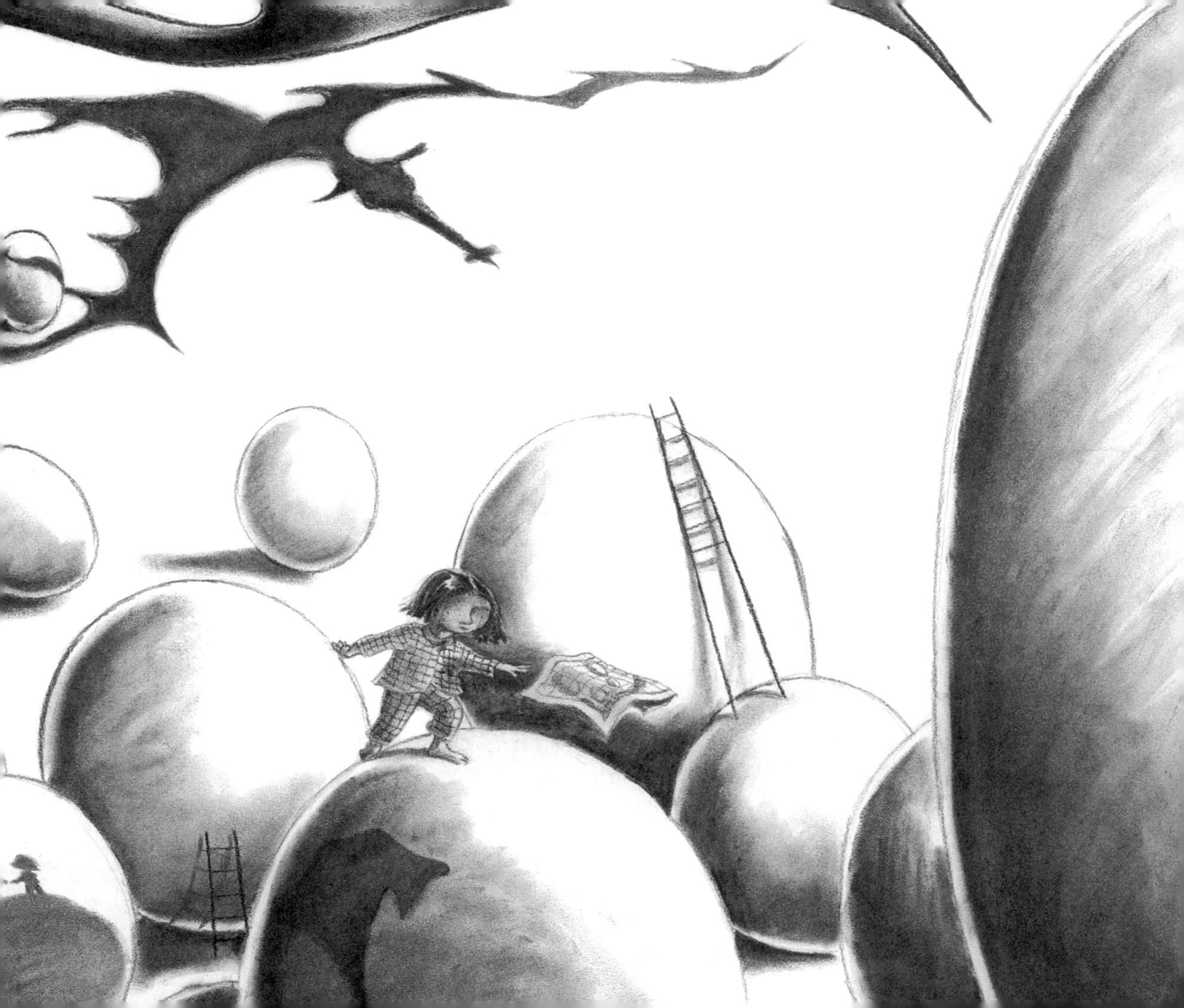

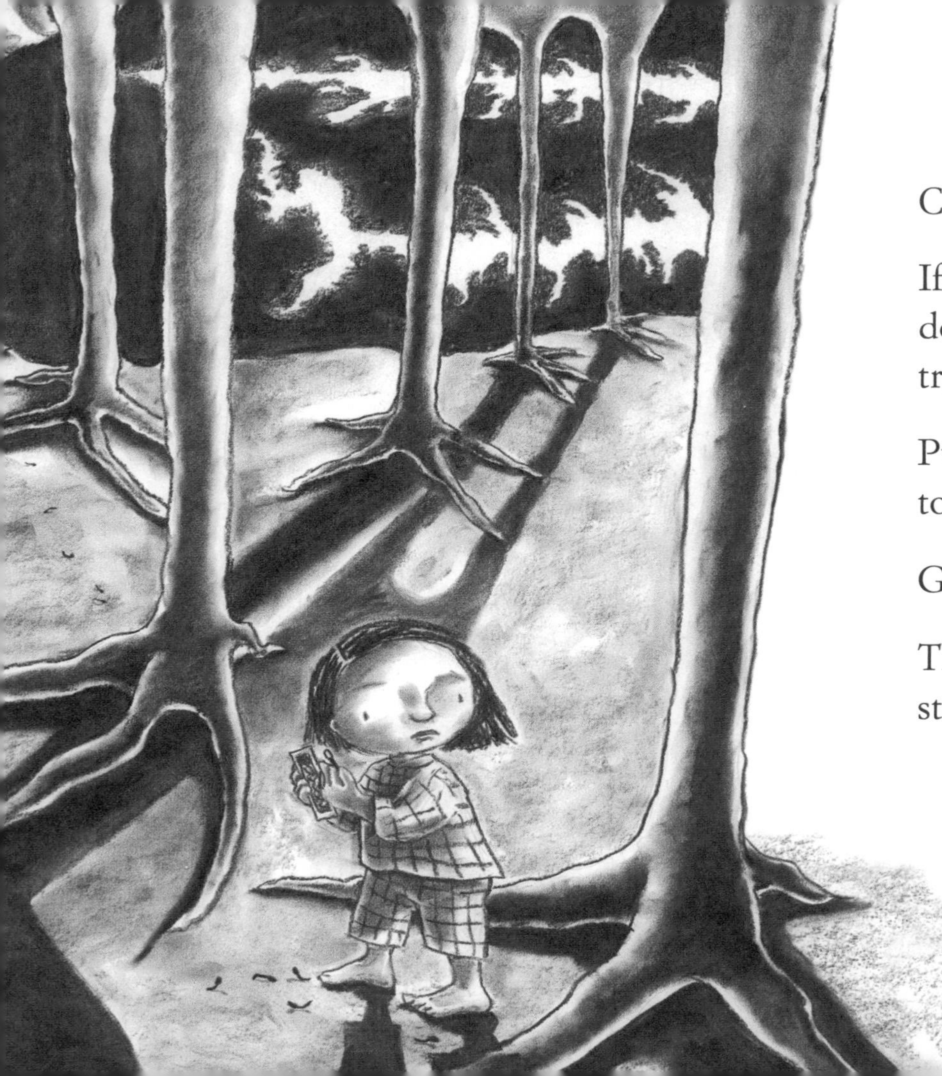

Chin up.

If at first you
don't succeed,
try, try again.

Pull yourself
together.

Get a grip.

Think of the
starving millions.

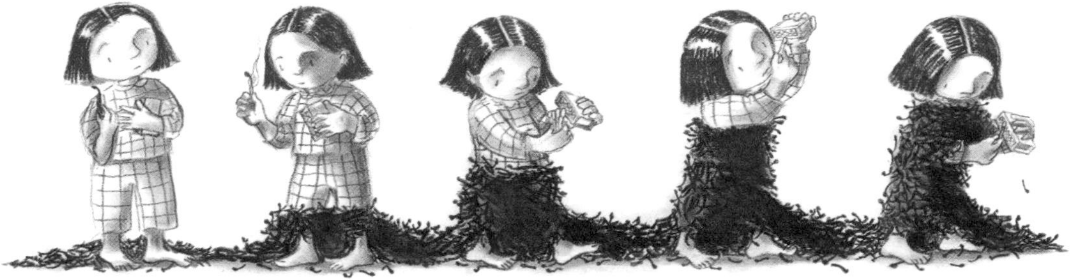

It is better to light a candle than curse the darkness.

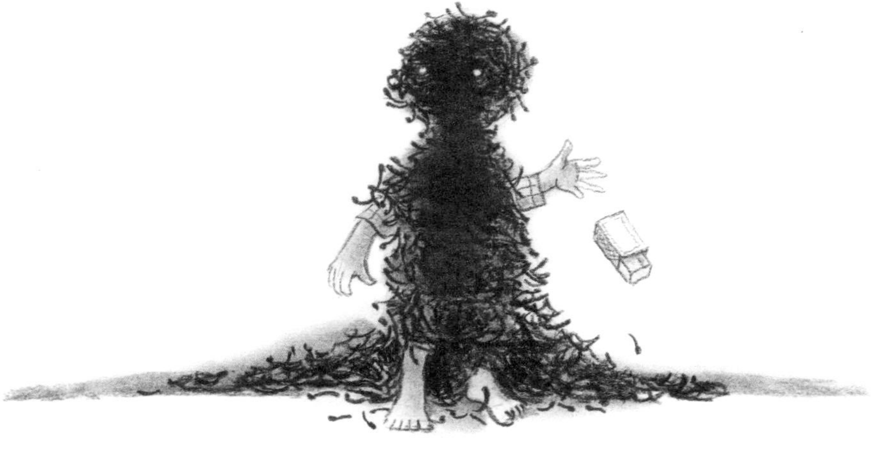

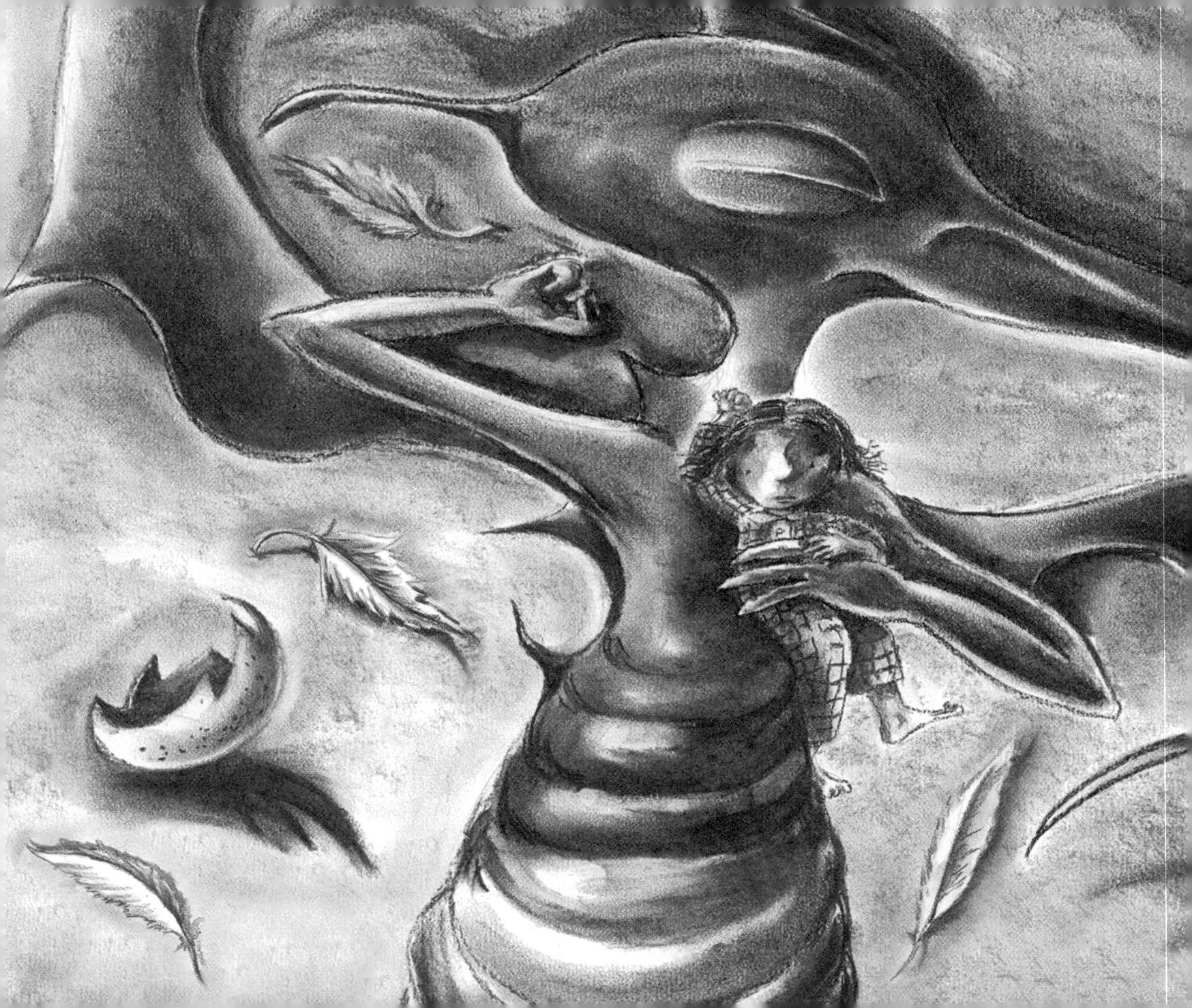

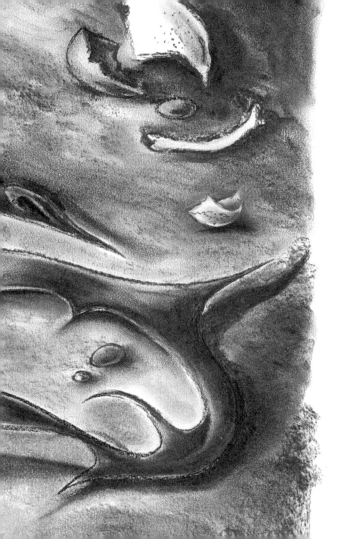

Night
skills:
the
ability
to
survive
inside
my
own
darkness.

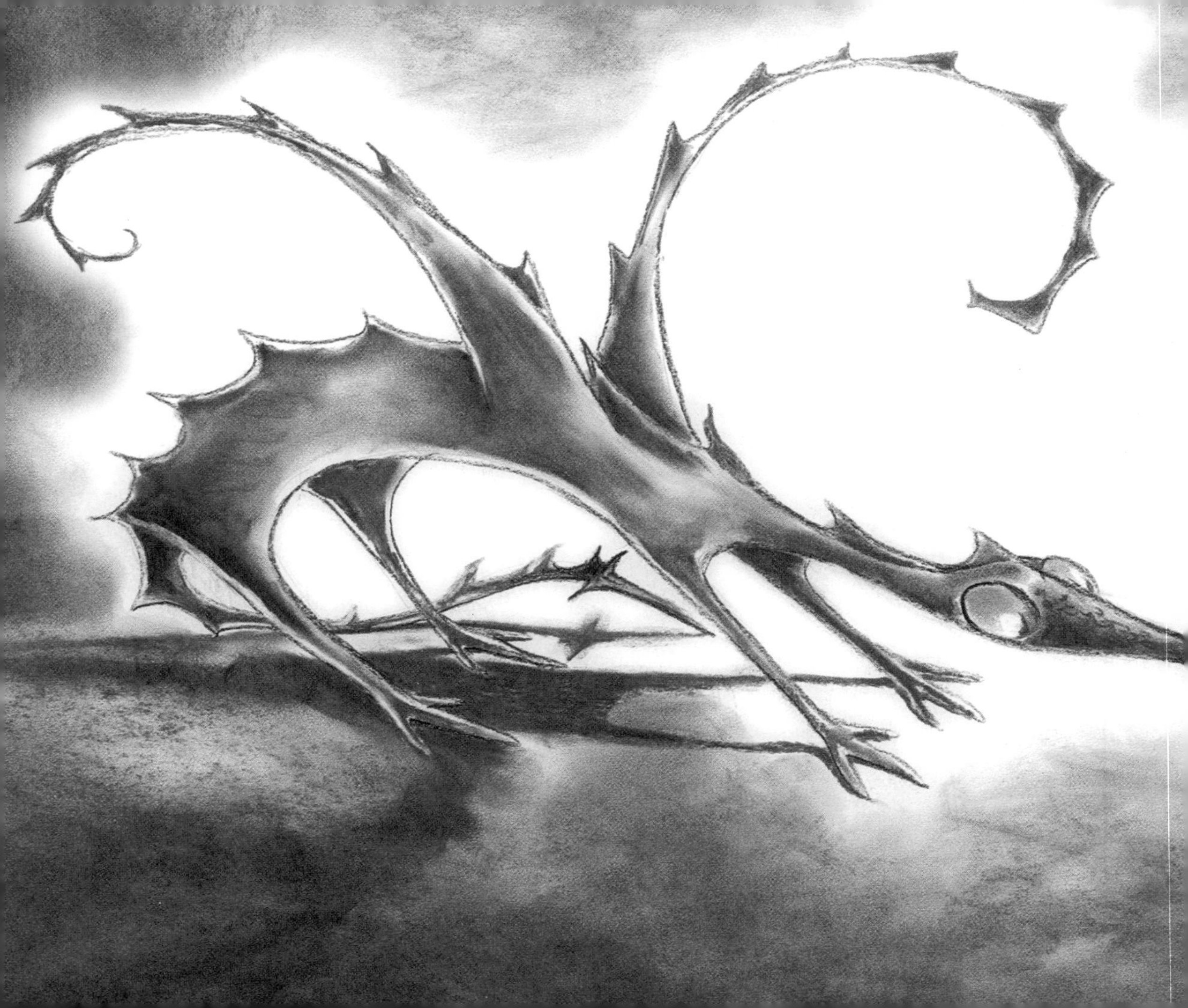

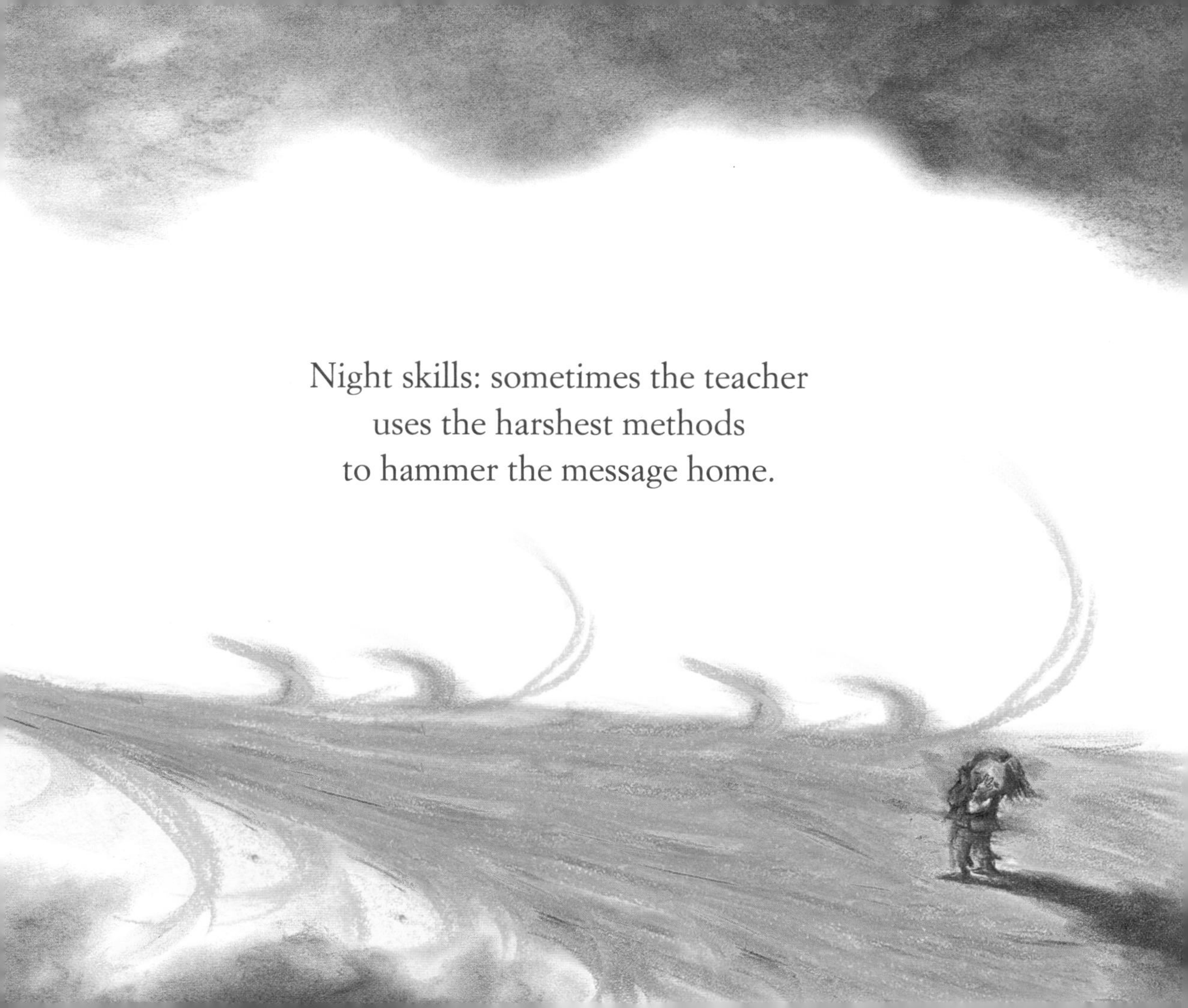

Night skills: sometimes the teacher
uses the harshest methods
to hammer the message home.

Night
skills:
holding
fast
to
nothing
in
the
knowledge
that
nothing
will
last
forever.

And one day I dragged myself out to run, with the dragons not far behind, reminding me this was pointless, that I couldn't possibly outrun them, and that I was too weak to even think about trying.

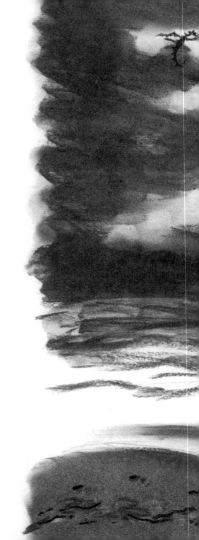

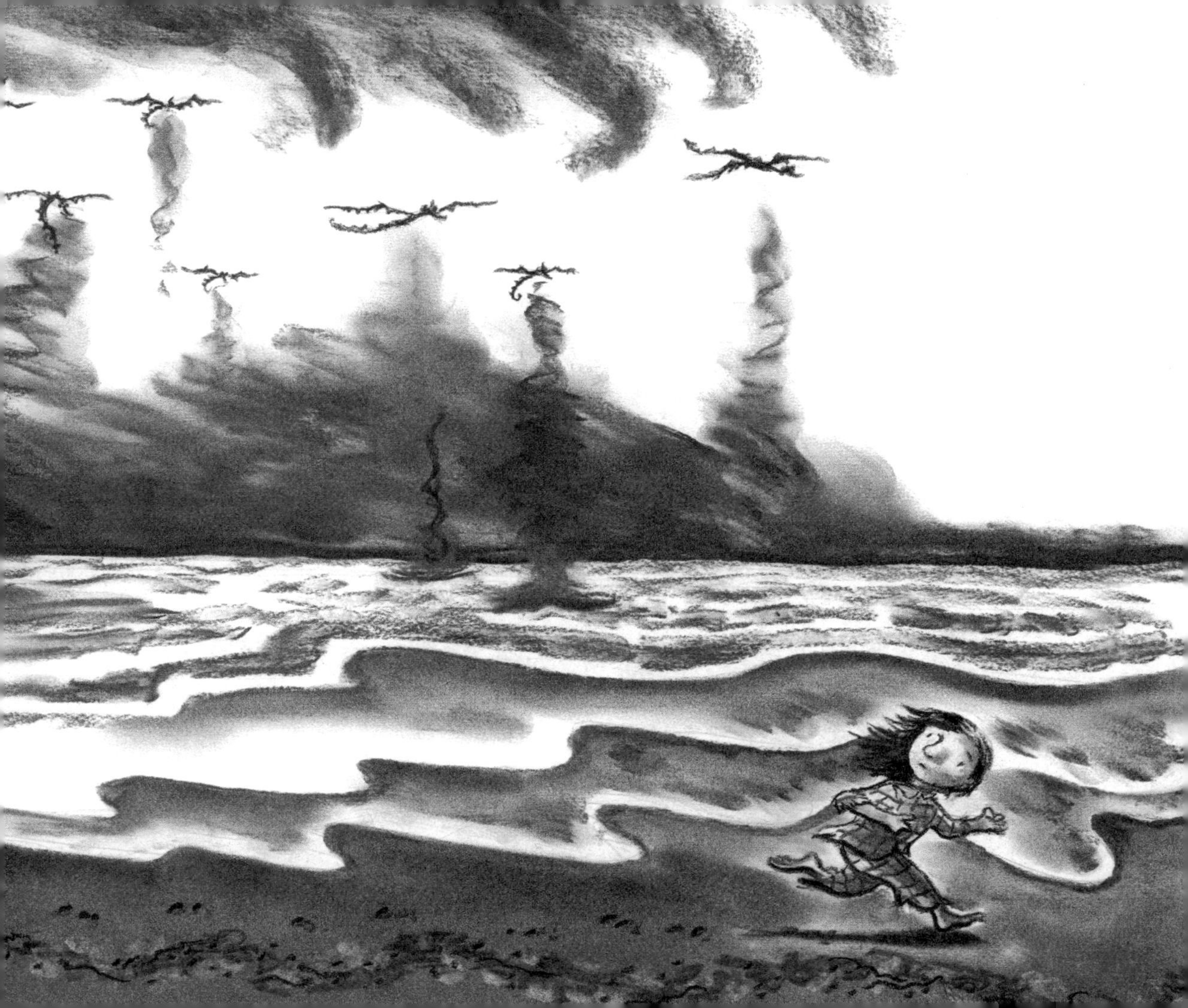

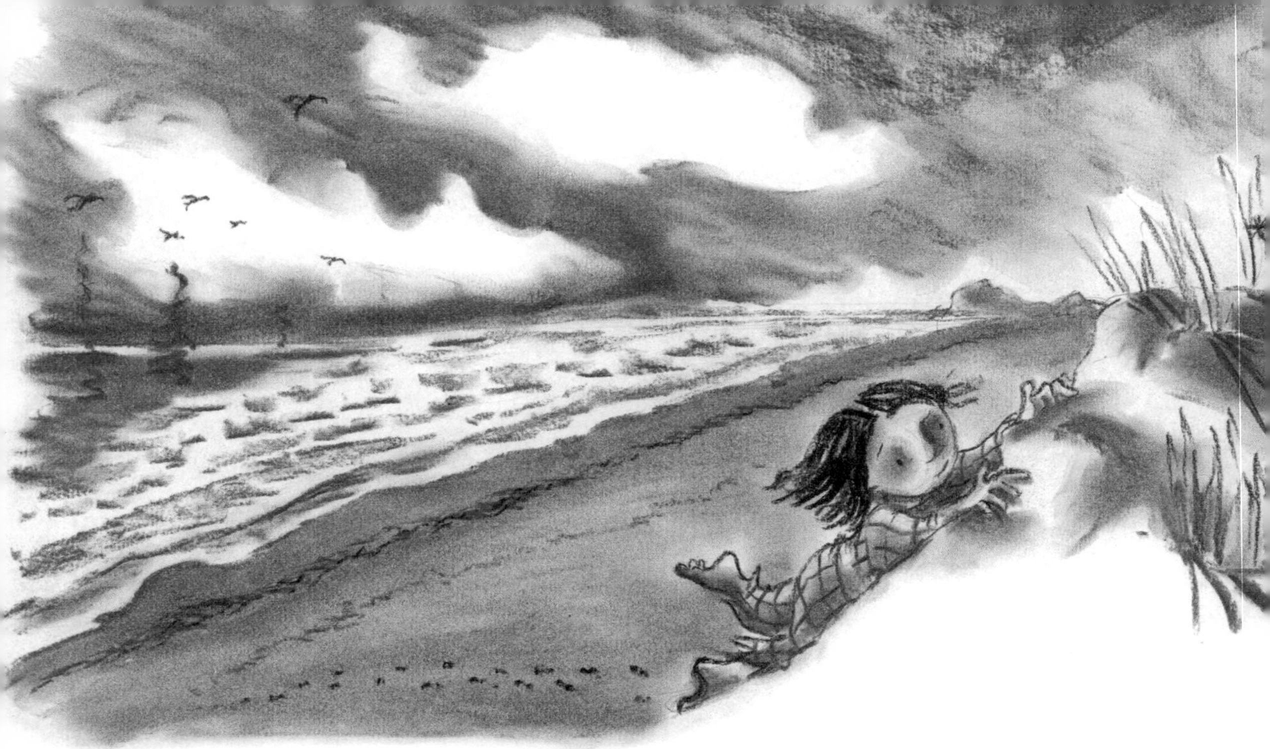

And then this happened. I couldn't run any more.
Out of breath. The dragons were right. I was weak.
I dragged myself up on top of a sand dune.

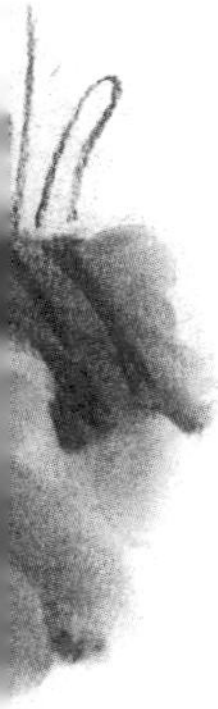

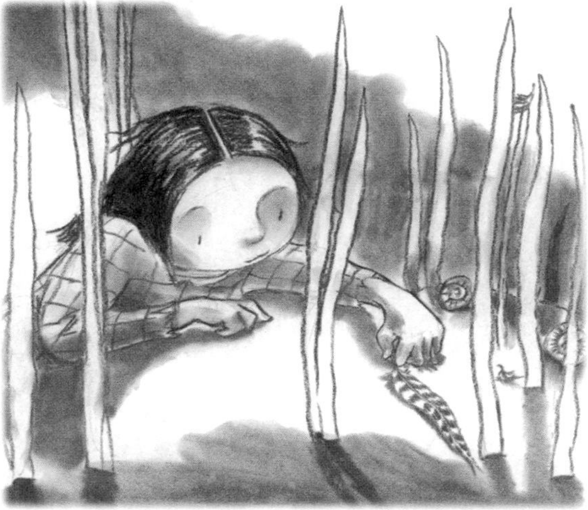

And there lying in the grass was a feather.
Black and white. Stripy and beautiful.
Neither black, nor all white.

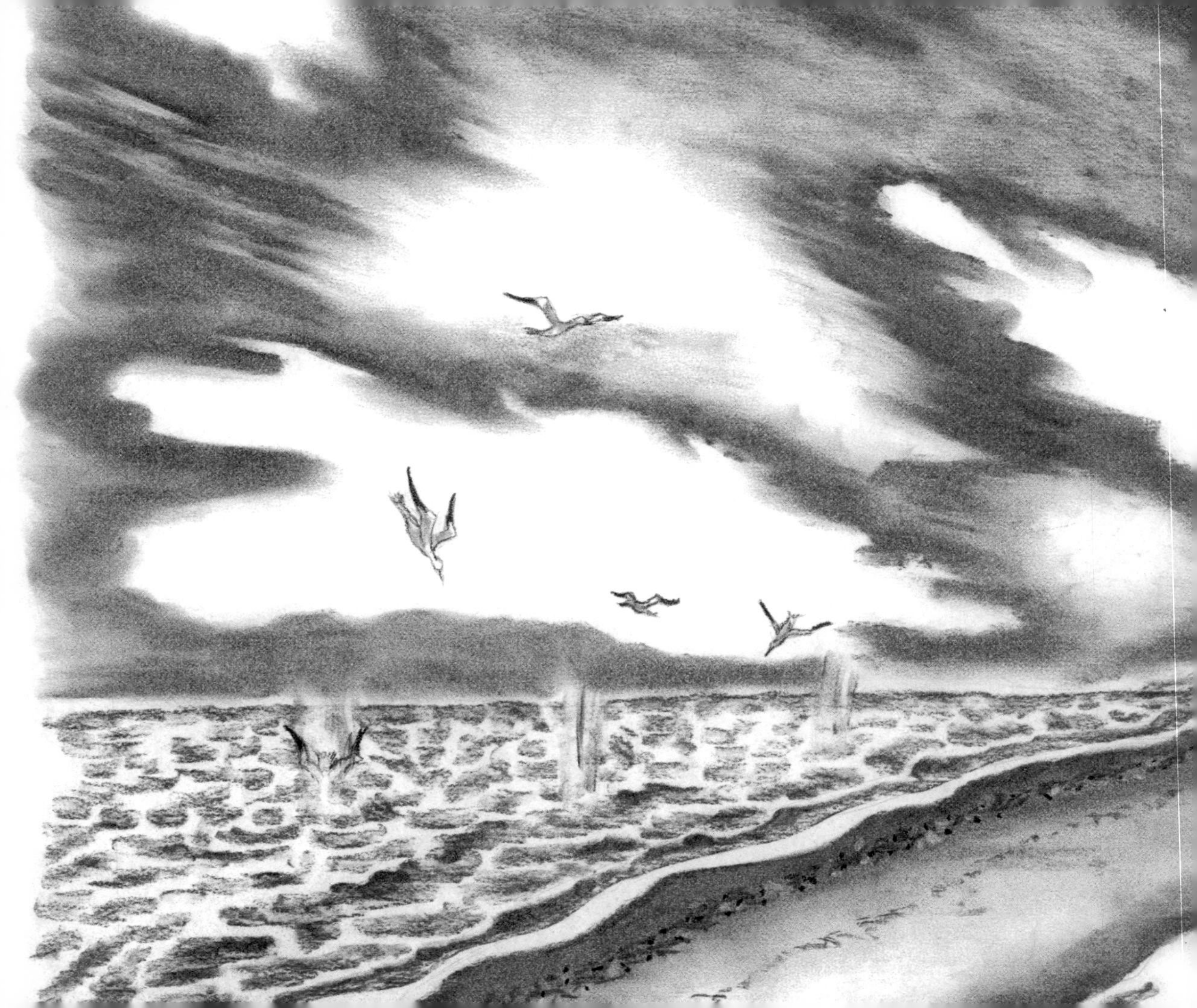

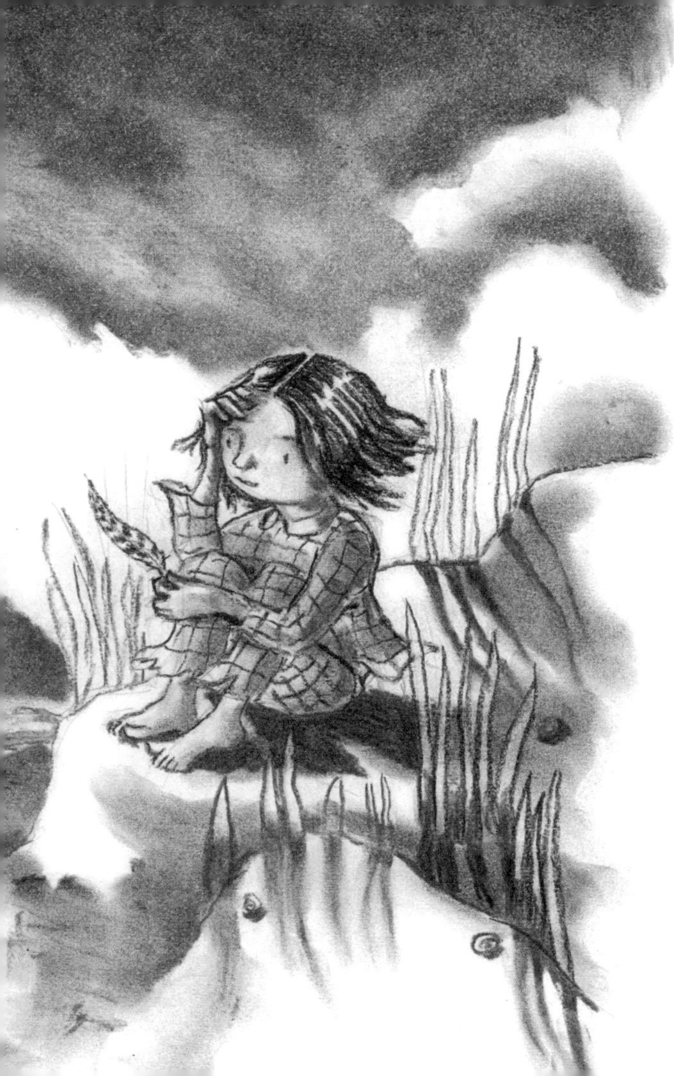

And something shifted.

This book is the result of spending most of my adult life living through periods of depressive illness. Some of these have been severe enough to warrant medical intervention, others have eventually responded to counseling, and sometimes I have simply hung on and waited to become well again.

It is almost impossible to describe the territory of depression; in doing so, we resort to metaphors. We speak of the gray fog, the black dog, or the downward spiral. When we are in the throes of the severest forms of this illness, many of us are hardly able to speak at all, far less articulate how we feel. This inability to put into words what we're experiencing is why I have used images to illustrate this bleak territory. While it hardly needs saying that these reflect my personal experience of depression, I hope that the drawings convey the real anguish suffered by the one in five of us who live with this illness.

I have used dragons to represent depression. This is partly because of their legendary ability to turn a fertile realm into a blackened, smoking ruin and partly because popular mythology shows them as monstrous opponents with a tendency to pick fights with smaller creatures. I'm not particularly brave or resourceful, and after so many years of combat I have to admit to a certain weariness, but I will arm-wrestle dragons for eternity if it means that I can help anyone going through a similar struggle.

And that is where you, Gentle Reader, come in. Being ill and unable to communicate how we feel is such a lonely business. My hope is that this book will help explain what we're going through.

Debi Gliori